THE CONIFEROUS FOREST BIOME

Enslow Publishing
101 W. 23rd Street
Suite 240
New York, NY 10011
USA

enslow.com

Colin Grady

WORDS TO KNOW

bogs—Lands that are wet and soggy.

climate—The weather conditions in a place over a period of years.

community—A group of living things that share the same area.

coniferous—Having cones rather than fruit or flowers.

hibernation—Spending the winter in deep sleep.

lichens—Small plants that often grow on rocks and look like moss.

logging—Cutting down trees into logs and getting them out of the forest.

shrubs—Low, bushy plants.

temperature—How hot or cold something is.

wetlands—Land that has a lot of water in the soil.

CONTENTS

Coniferous forest biomes are found in the northern parts of the world.

The Coniferous Forest Biome

A biome is a community of plants and animals that live together in a certain place and climate. There are many different biomes, such as deserts and grasslands. Another kind of biome is the coniferous forest.

The coniferous forest is the largest biome on land. The coniferous forest biome is found in the northern parts of Asia, Europe, and North America. This biome makes up one-third of the world's forests.

What Is a Coniferous Tree?

Most of the trees in coniferous forests are conifers. Instead of growing leaves and flowers, conifers grow needles

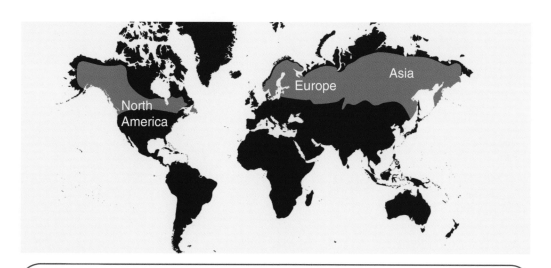

The areas in blue show where the world's coniferous forests are located.

and cones. Conifer means "to grow cones" in the Latin language.

Conifers are also called evergreens. Unlike other trees, most evergreens keep their needles or leaves all year long.

Seasons in the Coniferous Forest

Winters in most coniferous forests are long, cold, and snowy. Summers are usually short and warm. The temperature ranges from

Most conifers grow thin needles that stay on the trees year-round.

about –40 degrees Fahrenheit to about 68 degrees Fahrenheit (–40 degrees Celsius to 20 degrees Celsius). Most coniferous forests get about 12 to 35 inches (30 to 89 centimeters) of rain each year. Some get as much as 79 inches (200 centimeters) of rain a year.

Bodies of Water

Water comes in many forms in a coniferous forest. Some coniferous forests have bogs, shallow lakes, rivers, or wetlands. These bodies of water are important for the trees, plants, and animals that live there.

Many Names

Coniferous forests are also known as boreal forests. *Boreal* means "northern." They are also called taiga, which means "marshy pine" in the Russian language.

Bogs are wetlands that hold rainwater. Some bogs have been around for thousands of years.

Coniferous Trees and Plants

How do coniferous trees survive long, snowy winters? Their cone shape helps them! When snow or ice sticks to branches, it can get very heavy and the branches can snap off the trees. But the coniferous tree's cone shape does not let lots of snow and ice gather on the branches. Also, through the year the tree's needles are able to take in heat from the sun.

The shape of coniferous trees protects them from snow and ice.

Small Plants

The trees of the coniferous forest stop a lot of sunlight from getting to the forest floor. Still, small plants do grow there. Some plants grow on the ground while others grow on tree trunks. Shrubs, mosses, and lichens make up much of the plant life in the coniferous forest.

The Benefits of Bark

Many coniferous trees grow thick bark that protects them during cold winters. The thick bark also protects the trees from small wildfires.

Low plants cover the floor of the coniferous forest.

Wildlife in the Coniferous Forest

The coniferous forest is home to many animals. These animals have different ways of getting through the long winters. Some have layers of fat, fur, or feathers that keep them warm. Other animals just sleep all the way through winter! This is called hibernation. This helps the animals since it is hard to find food in the winter.

Many animals of the forest, such as this black bear, hibernate during the cold winter months.

Don't Wake That Bear!

Bears don't go into a truly deep sleep during their hibernation. It's more like a light sleep during which they do not eat or drink for about six months. But they are easily woken, so don't ever bother a hibernating bear!

Birds in the Coniferous Forest

The coniferous forest is also home to many different birds, such as woodpeckers, ravens, owls, and hawks. Most of these birds make their homes in the branches of coniferous trees.

When the weather gets too cold or food runs out, many birds move to warmer areas.

At Home in the Coniferous Forest

The coniferous forest is home to small communities of people. Many of them have jobs or hobbies having to do with the forest. People living in a coniferous forest might be hunters or they might fish in the many bodies of water found there. Others might make a living by logging, which means cutting down trees to be used for important things, such as paper, furniture, and houses.

Today many forests are being chopped down. People use wood for many things, but we must make sure that we keep plenty of trees in the forests.

Helpful Trees

Did you know that trees are important to the air that you breathe? Trees give off oxygen, which animals and humans need to breathe. So we need lots of trees in order to live. This is just one more reason to protect our trees!

Losing Our Trees

The coniferous forest can be harmed when people cut down too many trees. Many animals lose their homes when this happens. The animals often cannot find new places to live or enough food to eat. Also, pollution in the air can harm our forests.

We must take care of the forests. The coniferous forest biome is important to many kinds of life.

Many trees, plants, and animals call the coniferous forest their home.

ACTIVITY
SAVE THE CONIFEROUS FOREST

You learned in this book about the plants and wildlife that live in the coniferous forest. You also learned that some of these forests are in danger because people cut them down or pollution hurts them. Let's make a poster to get people to save our trees.

1. At the top of a large piece of blank paper or poster board, write a title, such as "Save the Evergreens!" Underneath your title, write a sentence or two about one of the dangers that faces coniferous forests, such as cutting down too many trees or pollution.

2. Now draw four large squares (see the example on page 23).

3. In each of the four squares, write one reason why the coniferous forest is important. You might want to list the different animals and plants that live there or explain why the coniferous forest is different

Save the Evergreens!

The coniferous forest is in danger because air pollution from factories hurts the trees. These forests are important because:

Birds like cardinals live in trees.

from other forests. Illustrate each of your reasons for saving the coniferous forests with a drawing or print out pictures from the Internet.

4. Hang up your poster in your classroom so your classmates can learn about these important forests.

LEARN MORE

Books

Bow, James. *Forests Inside Out*. New York: Crabtree, 2015.

Duke, Shirley. *Seasons of the Boreal Forest Biome*. Vero Beach, FL: Rourke, 2014.

Fleisher, Paul. *Forest Food Webs*. Minneapolis: Lerner, 2013.

Johansson, Philip. *The Taiga: Discover This Forested Biome*. New York: Enslow, 2015.

Websites

Skyenimals: Coniferous Forest
www.skyenimals.com/browse_habitat.cgi?habitat=coniferous_forest
Includes information and photos of the animals of the coniferous forest.

Kids Do Ecology: World Biomes
kids.nceas.ucsb.edu/biomes/taiga.html
Photos, facts, and links to information about the taiga.

INDEX

Published in 2017 by Enslow Publishing, LLC.
101 W. 23rd Street, Suite 240, New York, NY 10011

Copyright © 2017 by Enslow Publishing, LLC

Library of Congress Cataloging-in-Publication Date
Names: Grady, Colin, author.
Title: The coniferous forest biome / Colin Grady.
Description: New York, NY : Enslow Publishing, [2017] | Series: Zoom in on biomes | Includes bibliographical references and index.
Identifiers: LCCN 2015048567| ISBN 9780766077461 (library bound) | ISBN 9780766077430 (pbk.) | ISBN 9780766077454 (6-pack)
Subjects: LCSH: Taigas--Juvenile literature. | Taiga ecology--Juvenile literature. | Conifers--Juvenile literature. | Forest ecology--Juvenile literature. | Forests and forestry--Juvenile literature.

Classification: LCC QH541.5.T3 S86 2016 | DDC 577.3/7--dc23
LC record available at http://lccn.loc.gov/2015048567

Printed in Malaysia

To Our Readers: We have done our best to make sure all website addresses in this book were active and appropriate when we went to press. However, the author and the publisher have no control over and assume no liability for the material available on those websites or on any websites they may link to. Any comments or suggestions can be sent by e-mail to customerservice@enslow.com.

Photo Credits: Cover, p. 1 Wild Horizon/Universal Images Group/Getty Images; throughout book, ashuk/DigitalVision Vectors/Getty Images (tree background), Kathy Konkle/DigitalVision Vectors/Getty Images (tree, pinecone, bear, and squirrel graphics); p. 4 Fotosearch/Getty Images; p. 6 Designua/Shutterstock.com; p. 7 iStock.com/bgwalker; p. 9 Dean van't Schip/All Canada Photos/Getty Images; p. 11 STOCK4B/Getty Images; p. 13 Lanaw/Shutterstock.com; p. 15 John E Marriott/All Canada Photos/Getty Images; p. 17 MARSHFIELD PHOTOGRAPHY/ EILEEN FONFERKO/Moment Open/Getty Images; p. 19 sunlow/iStock/Thinkstock; p. 21 kavram/Shutterstock.com; p. 23 (top left) iStock.com/SteveByland.